◆ Personal, Moral, Social and Cultural education

GROWING UP TODAY
Dealing with problems

Key Stage 1/P1-3

Ros Bayley and Lynn Broadbent

HOPSCOTCH EDUCATIONAL PUBLISHING

◆ Acknowledgements

Published by Hopscotch Educational Publishing Company Ltd,
Althorpe House, Althorpe Street, Leamington Spa CV31 2AU.

© Hopscotch Educational Publishing

Written by Ros Bayley and Lynn Broadbent
Cover design by Kim Ashby
Page design by Steve Williams
Illustrated by Cathy Gilligan
Cover illustration by Cathy Gilligan
Printed by Clintplan, Southam

Ros Bayley and Lynn Broadbent hereby assert their moral right to be identified as the authors of this work in accordance with the Copyright, Designs and Patents Act, 1988.

ISBN 1-902239-17-2

All rights reserved. This book is sold subject to the condition that it shall not, by way of trade or otherwise, be lent, hired out or otherwise circulated without the publisher's prior consent in any form or binding or cover other than that in which it is published and without a similar condition, including this condition, being imposed upon the subsequent purchaser.

No part of this publication may be reproduced, stored in a retrieval system, or transmitted, in any form or by any means, electronic, mechanical photocopying, recording or otherwise, without the prior permission of the publisher, except where photocopying for educational purposes within the school or other educational establishment that has purchased this book is expressly permitted in the text.

Contents

Introduction	4
Feeling undervalued	6
Facing challenges	11
Resolving conflict	16
Peer group pressure	21
Coping with prejudice	26
Working together to solve problems	31
Making difficult choices	36
Taking responsibility	41

Generic sheets
Five facts about problems	46
Our problems	47

Acknowledgements	48

A complete list of the children's storybooks referred to in this book, together with authors and publishers

Introduction

Facing up to problems and challenges is difficult enough for adults but for young children such situations can often be intensely painful. As they begin to realise that life is not always the way they might want it to be, they need our support and help in coping with the difficulties and challenges that are an unavoidable part of daily life.

Through the medium of story, we can provide young children with a safe context for exploring and reflecting upon the range of difficulties they are likely to encounter.

In selecting the books that form the basis for work in this area, we have endeavoured to focus on the problems that, in our experience, most commonly affect the lives of young children. Through exploring the circumstances and events that surround the characters in the stories it is our hope that, with adult help and support, the children will be able to relate the issues to their personal experience and begin to understand that problems and difficulties are a natural part of many people's lives. What we really want is for them to be able to develop a positive attitude to problems and to see them as opportunities for learning. This will not happen instantly and will need help from the adults who work with them. Those adults should, of course, be sensitive to the individual situations of the children and ensure that any work on these topics does not cause distress.

Children learn by example and if we as adults can demonstrate an ability to deal positively with problems that we face, we can be powerful role models. Obviously, there are certain experiences that it would not be appropriate for us to share with the children but if we can help them to see that our own lives involve us in dealing with a wide variety of problems this can be extremely beneficial.

In our efforts to protect children, we often deny what is happening to them and try to wave a magic wand that will make their troubles go away. This is always done with the best of intentions but ultimately does little to prepare them for the experiences they will need to deal with. If we can acknowledge the difficulties that children encounter we can really help them to face up to the situations they find themselves in and help them to learn to deal with problems sensitively, realistically and resourcefully.

The chapters in this book cover everday difficulties that children may experience, such as how it feels to fall out with their friends and how to face challenges at school.

At the other end of the continuum, we have chosen books that facilitate the exploration of more difficult issues, such as resisting peer group pressure, feeling undervalued and coping with prejudice.

Feeling undervalued

FOCUS BOOK

TALL INSIDE
by Jean Richardson and
Alice Englander
Picture Puffins

INTENDED LEARNING

◆ To help children to value themselves and others for who they are and not what they look like.
◆ To enable them to see themselves as unique individuals.

ANTICIPATED OUTCOMES

◆ They will understand that we are all different, that many of us feel unhappy about our physical appearance but they will learn that we are all special.

Synopsis of the story

Joanne is having great difficulty coming to terms with being the shortest person in her class. Nobody seems to understand how she feels and she becomes really upset when her friends start a club and she cannot join. To join the club you have to be able to jump up and swing from the branch of a tree and Joanne, who just cannot reach, ends up running home in floods of tears. Then she meets Lofty, the street clown, who not only acknowledges her feelings but helps her to see that there are some advantages to being small.

Notes for teachers

We have all, at one time or another, suffered from low self-esteem and this can be very difficult for children, especially when they feel themselves to be in some way different from their peers. We all need to feel that we belong to our group and if we feel ourselves to be different in some way this can be very alienating. Through sharing Tall Inside with children, we can provide them with a vehicle for discussing issues of self-esteem and help them to see the importance of valuing themselves and others for who they are and not what they look like. It is important to help the children to understand that feelings of inadequacy are quite natural and that what is important is how we deal with these feelings. It is all too easy to brush these feelings aside and not fully acknowledge them but if we can really hear children's concerns about how they feel about themselves we can help them towards a positive attitude to such feelings and an acceptance of their own individuality and uniqueness.

Methodology

The following key questions and points for consideration may be of assistance when working with this story.

Questions to ask

◆ Draw the children's attention to the illustrations on the first two pages of the book. Ask them: "How do you think Joanne felt about being the shortest person in her class?"

◆ Joanne's family tried to help her by making jokes about her size. Did this help her? How did she feel about what they said to her?

◆ When Jenny's cousins came to play they wouldn't let Joanne join the club because she couldn't reach the branch and swing from the tree. Ask: "When this happened, how did Joanne feel? Can you think of some words to describe her feelings?"

◆ Encourage children to relate what happened to their own experiences. Ask them: "Have you ever felt rejected or left out?" If they are willing, encourage them to share their experiences.

◆ Joanne was desperate to help Lofty in the ring. To help the children understand this, ask: "Why didn't Lofty see Joanne? When this happened, what did she do?" This may help them to see that because of her height Joanne had to be more determined than the other children.

◆ How did Joanne feel when she was all dressed up as a clown and parading around the ring?

◆ When the show was over, Joanne didn't want to take off her clown outfit. Why?

◆ To help the children understand how Joanne saw Lofty ask:
  – "Why was Joanne so surprised when Lofty climbed into the van?"
  – "How do you think that Joanne felt when Lofty told her that he didn't mind being short?"
  – "Why do you think that Joanne slept with the red nose under her pillow?"
  – "What do you think Jenny learned from meeting Lofty?"

The photocopiable activity sheets

My name This sheet is intended to provide the children with an opportunity to really focus on themselves. Some prior discussion will enable them to identify characteristics and interests relating to themselves which they can then incorporate into their design.

This is me In this activity the children focus on their physical appearance. It requires no writing and can be undertaken by children at all stages of development. Discussion of the completed sheets should help the children to understand and appreciate their own uniqueness.

The way I am This sheet is intended for children at a more advanced stage of development. It requires reflective thinking and the ability to write independently.

◆ My name ◆

- Create a design using your name. Draw a picture of yourself by your design.

Border decoration featuring names: Calum, BETH, Jack, ZOE, LIAM, Molly, ISAAC, Jasmine, AYSHA, Sam, LUCY, BEN, Caitlin, HANIF, PARMINDER, Joe

◆ This is me ◆

◆ Think about what you look like. Write your name and draw parts of yourself in these boxes.

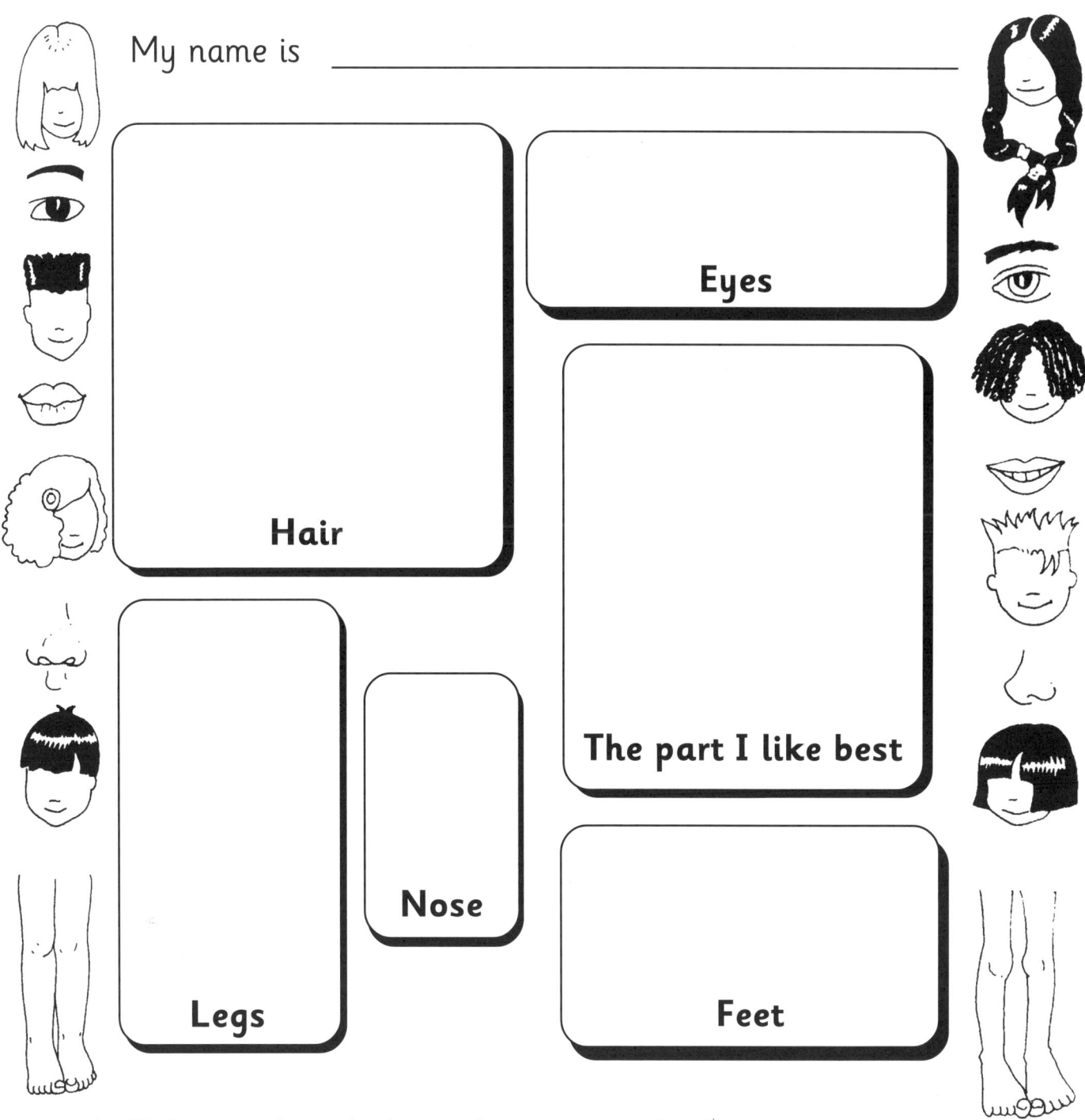

My name is _____

- Hair
- Eyes
- The part I like best
- Legs
- Nose
- Feet

◆ Talk to a friend about the way you look.

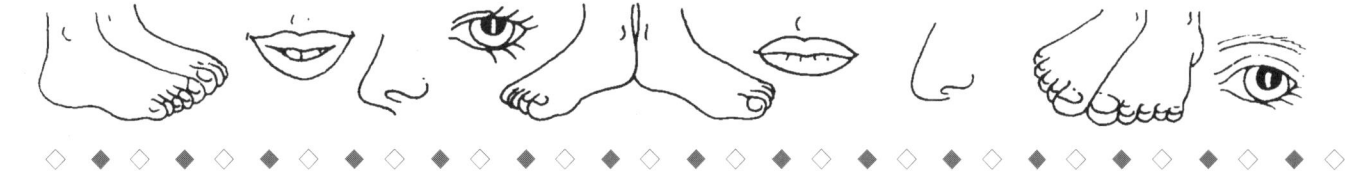

Hopscotch ◆ Dealing with problems KS1/P1–3   PHOTOCOPIABLE PAGE

◆ The way I am ◆

◆ Draw yourself in the box.

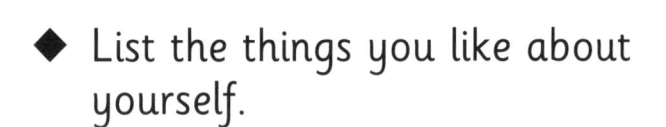

This is me

◆ List the things you like about yourself.

◆

◆

◆

◆

◆

◆

◆ Write about something about yourself that you would like to change if you could.

_____

_____

_____

_____

Facing challenges

FOCUS BOOK

PASS IT, POLLY
by Sarah Garland
Puffin

INTENDED LEARNING

◆ To help the children understand that hard work and determination are often a necessary part of achieving a goal.

ANTICIPATED OUTCOMES

◆ The children will understand that success has to be worked for. They will be able to name and talk about some of the qualities necessary for success.

Synopsis of the story

When Mr Budd invites his class to take part in a school football match, Polly and Nisha are the only girls who want to play. They turn up to the practices full of enthusiasm, only to be find that football wasn't as easy as they thought. Fortunately Nisha's grandad, who used to play football when he was in the army, turns out to be an excellent coach. He teaches them to tackle, dribble and score goals and on the day of the match they demonstrate their newly acquired skills.

Notes for teachers

Learning to stick at a task when things get difficult is never easy for any of us. Pass it, Polly provides us with an excellent resource for exploring this issue with young children. Through discussion of this story we can help them to see that there are times when we all have to be very determined if we want to succeed. We can help them to understand that enthusiasm on its own is not always enough and that success often requires application and hard work.

It is not always easy for children to acknowledge that they are finding things difficult and there are times when they would rather give up than admit to their difficulties. In sharing this story with them, we can help them to see the difficulties as opportunities for learning. What we really seek to communicate is that the real difference between someone who is successful and someone who is not is that the successful person keeps going when things get difficult. In this story, the girls persevere, even when the boys shout at them for being no good.

This book has been chosen for the opportunities it affords for discussing determination and perseverance but it can also involve us in looking at gender issues. It is interesting that when the girls want to play football the other girls are quite disparaging in their response. The author has cleverly omitted the responses of the boys but these may well surface when sharing the book with a group of children.

Methodology

The following questions and points for consideration may help the discussion of the story.

◆ When Polly and Nisha decide that they want to take part in the school football match it prompts a strong response from their friends. Explore this with the children by asking:
 – "What do Polly and Nisha's friends think about them wanting to be in the football team? Do they think it's a good idea? If not, why not?"
 – "At the first practice things don't go very well. Why do you think this is?"
 – "How do the boys behave towards Nisha and Polly?"
 – "How do Nisha and Polly feel at the end of the practice? Can you think of some words that would describe their feelings? What were the ways in which they tried to find out more about football?"

◆ As time went on Nisha and Polly felt very discouraged. When they spoke to Nisha's Mum what did she suggest? Why was this helpful? (The two girls recognised that they needed someone to teach them to play football.) Ask: "Have you ever wanted to learn to do something? Was it easy or difficult? Is there anything that you do that means that you need to practice regularly?"

◆ To help the children to understand the extent to which the girls persevered, ask them: "How many times did the girls go to Nisha's Grandad? Grandad taught them lots of skills. Can you remember what they were?"

◆ Encourage the children to relate the story to their own experiences. Ask them: "Have you ever found anything really difficult and wanted to give up?" It is also useful to share our own experience with them. Children are often quite surprised to realise that teachers can find things difficult! Explore Grandad's feelings by asking: "On the day of the match Grandad was one of the spectators. How do you think he felt when he was watching the match?"

◆ After the girls had lessons from Grandad they played really well. Ask: "How do you think they felt about this? What effect did this have on their friends?"

The photocopiable activity sheets

Difficult or easy? This sheet is designed to help the children to understand that what we find easy or difficult varies from person to person. It is suitable for children at all stages of development but will need plenty of follow up discussion in order to meet the objective.

A new skill This activity is aimed at helping the children to understand that learning a new skill involves hard work and application. Less developed children may need some support with writing their list.

Learning a new skill This sheet is designed for children who can read and write independently. They will need to refer back to the text when formulating their answers.

◆ Difficult or easy? ◆

◆ Cut out the pictures and sort them into two groups.
Group 1 – Things I think would be difficult to learn.
Group 2 – Things I think would be easy to learn.

Hopscotch ◆ Dealing with problems KS1/P1–3   PHOTOCOPIABLE PAGE

◆ A new skill ◆

◆ Draw a picture of something you would like to learn to do.

◆ List the things that you would need to do to help you to learn this new skill.

◆ _____

◆ _____

◆ _____

◆ _____

◆ Learning a new skill ◆

◆ The two girls in the story had to work hard to learn to play football. In these footballs, write the new things they had to learn.

Hopscotch ◆ Dealing with problems KS1/P1–3   PHOTOCOPIABLE PAGE   15

Resolving conflict

FOCUS BOOK

JAMAICA AND BRIANNA
by Juanita Havill and
Anne Sibley O'Brien
Mammoth

INTENDED LEARNING

◆ To help the children to understand that conflict is a natural part of any authentic relationship and that it is important to recognise it and deal with it honestly and positively.

ANTICIPATED OUTCOMES

◆ The children will see that we all have to deal with conflict and will be able to talk about and begin to deal with times when they have found themselves in conflict situations.

Synopsis of the story

Jamaica is horrified at having to wear her brother's hand-me-down boots and things become even worse when her friend Brianna laughs at them. To make her mother buy her some new boots, Jamaica pulls a hole in the toe until the boots become unwearable and she is able to have new ones. She goes to town and chooses some new boots that look just like cowboy boots. Unfortunately, when she wears them the next day, Brianna tells her that cowboy boots 'aren't in'. Jamaica is very hurt and, by way of retaliation, tells Brianna that she saw some pink boots like hers but didn't buy them because they were ugly. The conflict is not resolved until Brianna kicks off her boots and says she doesn't like them because they are her sister's old ones. Jamaica empathises and they become friends again.

Notes for teachers

We all, on occasions, have a tendency to run away from conflict situations; to regard such situations as negative and something to be brushed under the table. However, while this is understandable, it isn't exactly helpful. Conflict is a natural part of life and something that none of us can avoid. By fostering a positive attitude towards it we can really help children to deal with it honestly and openly. We can both create opportunities for growth and development and enhance the quality of our relationships.

The story of Jamaica and Brianna also provides us with an excellent platform for exploring issues around how what our friends think about things can really matter to us. It also presents us with a springboard for considering what it feels like to have to wear other people's hand-me-downs.

Methodology

The following key questions and points for consideration may be useful in discussing this story.

Questions to ask

- To set the scene, ask the children:
  – "Why do you think that Jamaica had to wear her brother's old boots? How do you think she felt about this? Can you think of any words to describe her feelings?"
- "When Jamaica was at the bus stop, why was she so worried about Brianna talking loudly? (It is important to help the children understand Jamaica's embarrassment. Encourage them to relate what happened to Jamaica to their own experience. If they are willing, allow them to share their experiences.)
- Jamaica deliberately made the hole in the boots bigger so that she would have to have new ones. Ask: "Was this a good idea? What would have happened if her Mum had not been able to buy new ones?"
- Jamaica really liked Brianna's pink boots, so why did she not buy some the same? To help the children understand how Jamaica's feelings change get them to compare the two illustrations of Jamaica going to the bus stop. Jamaica thinks that her new boots are beautiful and is surprised at Brianna's response. Ask: "Why do you think Brianna said that cowboy boots aren't in?"
- Jamaica described Brianna's boots as ugly. Ask: "Why do you think she said this?" (It's important to help the children to explore the way in which we often use put-downs when we feel hurt.) "How have Brianna's comments made Jamaica feel about having to wear her boots to school on Monday?"
- On Monday, Jamaica didn't speak to Brianna at the bus stop. "Why do you think this was? What has made Brianna dislike her pink boots so much?"
- When Jamaica hears Brianna say that her boots are her sister's ugly old boots, her attitude changes. "Why do you think this happens?"
- At the end of the story the two girls tell each other the truth. "What do they say to each other that they had not said before? What might have happened if they had not done this?"

The photocopiable activity sheets

What hurts and upsets you? This activity is aimed at helping the children to understand that we can be hurt and upset by different things. It is a speaking and listening activity and requires no writing.

How did they do it? This sheet is designed to help the children to understand that successful conflict resolution is dependent upon us engaging in a range of positive behaviours. Less developed children may need supporting in reading the sentences.

If this was you . . . This sheet asks the children to put themselves in the position of another child. It requires them to write independently but could be undertaken as a shared writing experience with less developed children.

FURTHER READING

- Mr Potter's Pigeon by Reg Cartwright (Hutchinson)
- The Selfish Giant by Oscar Wilde (There are many editions of this story.)

◆ What hurts and upsets you? ◆

◆ Look at these pictures. Put a ✔ by the things that would upset you.

◆ Compare your answers with a friend. What do you notice?

How did they do it?

◆ Look at these pictures. The two children have fallen out and then made friends again.

1

2

◆ Write some words about how the two boys feel:

In picture 1 _____

In picture 2 _____

◆ Draw a circle around the sentences that tell us what they did to sort out their problem.

- They hit each other.
- They listened to each other.
- They swore at each other.
- They talked to each other.
- They ignored each other.
- They said "sorry".

◆ If this was you . . . ◆

◆ How would you feel?

◆ Colour the boxes to show how you would feel.

| upset | angry | frustrated |

| anxious | embarrassed |

| hurt | worried | furious |

◆ Write a sentence about what you might say to these children.

_____
_____
_____
_____

Peer group pressure

FOCUS BOOK

HECTOR'S NEW TRAINERS
by Amanda Vesey
Picture Lions

INTENDED LEARNING

◆ To enhance understanding of peer group pressure and the way it makes people feel.
◆ To help children recognise that they can choose the extent to which they are influenced by peer group pressure.

ANTICIPATED OUTCOMES

◆ The children will recognise when peer group pressure is happening to them and be able to consider how they deal with it.

Synopsis of the story

Hector is very excited about his birthday and knows precisely what he wants for a present. He wants a pair of trainers exactly like his friends. Unfortunately, when he opens his parcel, he finds that the trainers are not the right ones. On the ankle collar, where there should have been a red football, there is a bright yellow star and when Hector wears his new trainers to the park he is ridiculed by his friends. As he plods sadly home, the bad boys seize him and attempt to pull off his new trainers thinking that they will be able to sell them. It is then that Leroy, the school hero, passes by on his skateboard and rescues Hector, who then invites him to his birthday party. When Leroy turns up at the party wearing the same trainers as Hector, Hector's trainers suddenly become very desirable!

Notes for teachers

Regardless of our age there are times when we all have to deal with peer group pressure and this can be extremely painful for young children.

To not have the right pair of trainers to wear or the right label on your school bag can cause enormous anxiety and embarrassment. Children can all too easily become victims of popular culture and media hype and as teachers we will frequently find ourselves having to deal with the unfortunate outcome of children not always having the right piece of merchandise.

There is very little we can do to change this situation but quite a lot we can do in terms of helping children cope with the situations they find themselves in. By doing so we can go a long way towards enabling them to cope with the even greater pressures they will encounter as they get older.

A child who can begin to recognise when he or she is being subjected to peer group pressure will find it a lot easier to cope when pressure is put on them to smoke, abuse substances, engage in substance abuse or engage in under-age sex. Exploring the issues of peer pressure in an early years' context can really help.

Methodology

The following key questions and points for consideration may be of assistance.

Questions to ask

- To help set the scene, ask the children: "Why did Hector want new trainers for his birthday? What did he think would happen if he got them?"; "Why was Hector so disappointed with his new trainers? Why was it so important to him that they had a red football on the ankle collar?".
- To help the children relate the story to their own experiences ask them: "Why did Hector want to be the same as everyone else? Does this happen in our school? Can you think of any ways that people in our school like to be the same? How do you think Hector's Mum and Dad felt when he didn't like his trainers? Why didn't they buy him the ones with the red football on the ankle collar?
- Hector had a lovely time in his new trainers until Gordon says that they are not the real thing. Ask: "How does this make him feel?"
- On the way home Hector meets the bad boys. Ask: "Why did they want his trainers?"
- Leroy liked Hector's trainers. Ask: "Do you think this changed the way that Hector felt about them?" When Leroy turned up at the party with the same trainers as Hector, Gordon wanted to swop trainers with Hector. "Why did he want to do this?"
- Hector liked his trainers when Leroy turned up in ones that were the same. Ask: "Do you think that he would have liked them as much if this had not happened?"

Let the children talk around the issues and relate the story to their own experiences. Ask them for their own ideas and comments about what they might do when they find themselves in similar situations to Hector.

The photocopiable activity sheets

Put the people into groups This sheet is intended to help the children in identifying peer groups. It is a cutting and sticking activity that is appropriate for a range of developmental levels.

Same or different? This sheet is aimed at encouraging the children to think about why they like to have certain 'trendy' things. It requires them to write one or two simple sentences.

Spot the difference This sheet will need to be supported by plenty of discussion to really help the children to understand the subtleties of peer group pressure. It is intended for the most developmentally able children.

◆ Put the people into groups ◆

◆ Sometimes people wear the same clothes to show that they belong together.

◆ Cut out the pictures and put them into three groups.

Group 1 – They go to the same school.

Group 2 – They do the same job.

Group 3 – They play for the same team.

Hopscotch ◆ Dealing with problems KS1/P1–3

Same or different?

◆ Put a ✔ by the pictures of the things that you have that are the same as your friends' things.

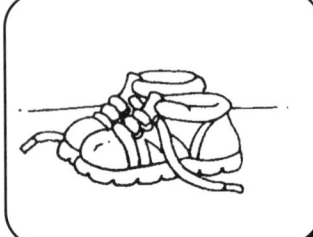

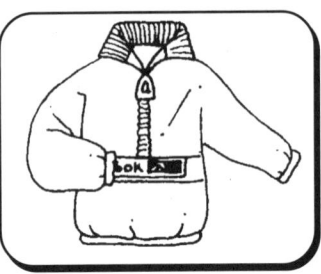

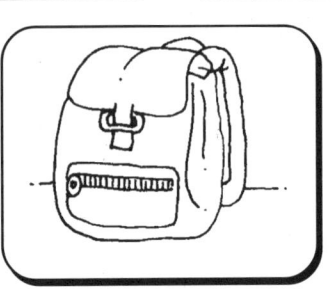

◆ Draw a picture of something that you have that is the same as your friends.

◆ Why is it important for it to be the same?

✎ _____
_____
_____
_____

◆ Spot the difference ◆

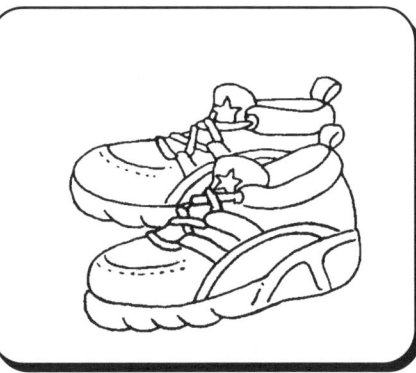

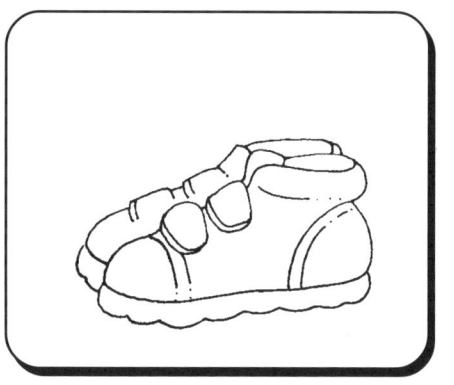

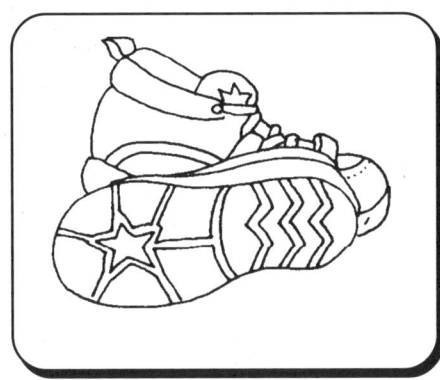

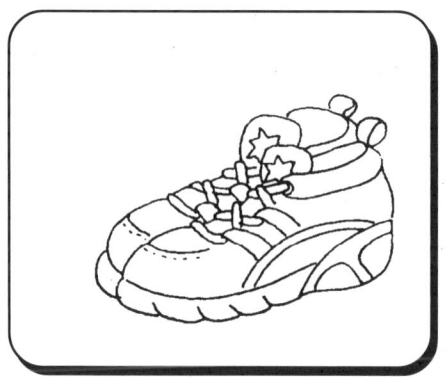

- ◆ This boy is crying because he has not got the 'right' trainers. Which of the trainers above are his? Colour them in.

- ◆ What could you say that might make him feel better?

✎ _____

_____

_____

_____

Hopscotch ◆ Dealing with problems KS1/P1–3   PHOTOCOPIABLE PAGE

◆ Coping with prejudice

FOCUS BOOK
AMAZING GRACE
by Mary Hoffman
and Caroline Birch
Frances Lincoln

INTENDED LEARNING

◆ To help children understand that self-belief and determination are important.
◆ To enable them to see that prejudice may be hurtful, but need not be a barrier to achievement.

ANTICIPATED OUTCOMES

◆ They will begin to see that determination is an important quality and understand what it means to be prejudiced.

Synopsis of the story

Grace loved stories and after she had heard them she would act them out. When her teacher announced that her class were to perform Peter Pan, she desperately wanted to play the part of Peter and became very sad when her friends said she couldn't. Peter, they told her, was a boy; she was a girl. They also pointed out that Peter Pan was not black. In spite of their comments, Grace still wanted to play the part and finally, with help and encouragement from her Mum and her Nana, she did.

Notes for teachers

Amazing Grace is a wonderful story for stimulating discussion around the issues of race, gender and self-belief.

When children come to school, they bring with them attitudes and beliefs that may already be deeply held and any challenge to such beliefs must be thoughtful and respectful. If they come from a background where racial prejudice exists, they will have absorbed such attitudes. As educators, it is our task to present them with alternative ways of seeing things. By the same token, if children live in family settings where males and females have traditionally stereotyped roles, then these will be the perceptions that they bring with them to school. The very least we can do is make them aware of the fact that not everyone sees things in this way and help them to see that within the school context there is a different value system to which they will be asked to conform.

In the story of Amazing Grace, we see the central character acting with courage and determination in spite of prejudice from her peers. This presents us with a wonderful opportunity for exploring the issue of self-belief and its role in achievement. By the time they come to school, most children will have experienced moments of self-doubt and it is extremely helpful for them to realise that everyone feels this some of the time.

The story portrays Grace within the context of a supportive family unit and helps children to appreciate the ways in which we all need the help and support of others.

Methodology

In discussing the story the following questions and points for consideration may prove useful.

Questions to ask

♦ To help the children understand Grace's enthusiasm for stories and drama, ask them: "Can you remember some of the stories that Grace acted out? What are some of the things she used to make the stories come to life? What sort of stories did she most like to act? Do you know any of the stories that Grace acted?"

♦ Her friends told her that because she was a girl and she was black, she couldn't be Peter Pan. Ask: "How do you think this made her feel? Did she let it put her off? Do you think her friends knew how she felt?"

♦ When Grace went home and told Mum what had happened, Mum started to get angry. Ask: "Why do you think she was angry?" Nana took Grace to the ballet. "Why do you think she did this? How do you think this helped Grace?" Point out that it was because of the support of her family that Grace overcame the prejudice.

♦ Clarify the children's understanding of audition before asking them: "Why did they have to have auditions for the part of Peter Pan? What did the children think about Grace when she tried for the part? Do you think she practised what she was going to say? How do you think she felt when the play was a great success?"

♦ Encourage the children to relate the story to their own experiences. Ask them: "What does it feel like when somebody tells you that they don't think you'll be able to do something? Have you ever surprised anybody by doing something that they said you couldn't?"

The photocopiable activity sheets

Who helps you? This activity is designed to assist the children in identifying their sources of help and support. It will need some preliminary discussion but is a simple activity intended for the less developmentally able.

What would you like to do? This activity is aimed at encouraging the children to expand their imaginations and focus on their ambitions as well as thinking about who might support them in this. It is intended for children who are beginning to write independently.

What can you do? This activity asks the children to focus on the things that they can do well. They need to be able to write a list and then a few short sentences about the person who helped them to do this.

◆ Who helps you? ◆

- ◆ Draw pictures of the people who help and support you to do the things you want.

- ◆ Write their names underneath.

PHOTOCOPIABLE PAGE   Hopscotch ◆ Dealing with problems KS1/P1–3

◆ What would you like to do? ◆

◆ Draw pictures to show two things that you would really like to do.

◆ Write a sentence about each one to explain why you would like to do it and who could help you.

Hopscotch ◆ Dealing with problems KS1/P1–3   PHOTOCOPIABLE PAGE   29

◆ What can you do? ◆

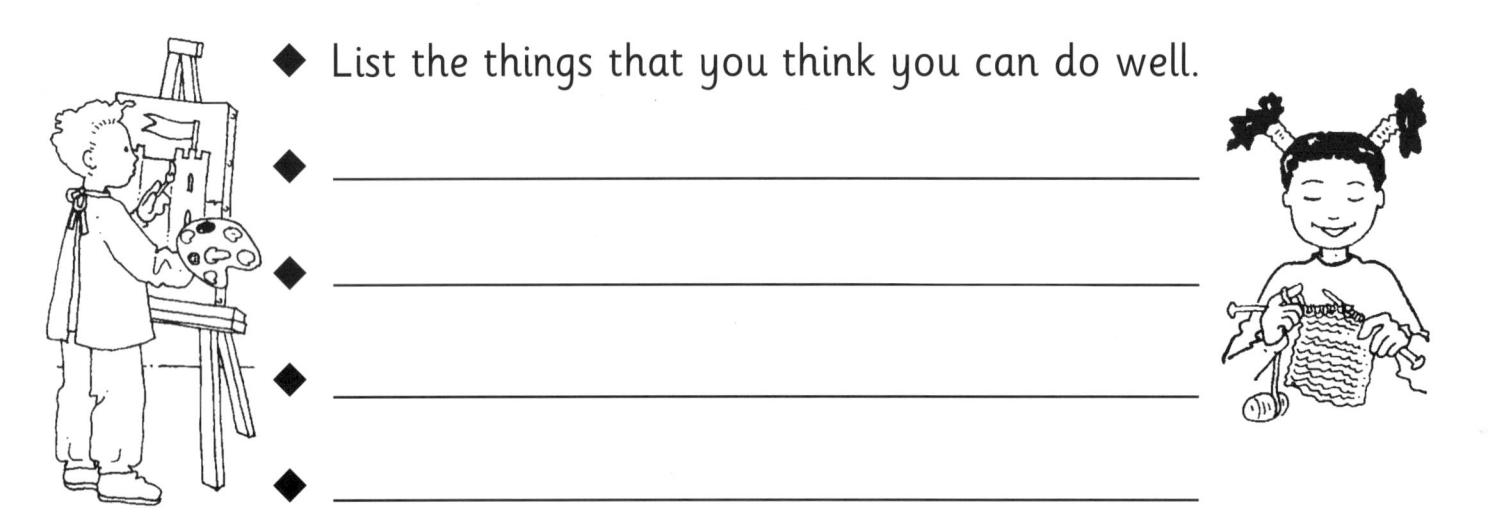

◆ List the things that you think you can do well.

◆ _____

◆ _____

◆ _____

◆ _____

◆ Draw a picture of yourself doing something that you are good at.

◆ Who helped you to learn to do this? Write about that person and how he or she helped you.

_____

_____

_____

_____

◆Working together to solve problems

FOCUS BOOK
OLD BEAR
by Jane Hissey
Arrow Books

INTENDED LEARNING

◆ To help children see that by working co-operatively we can solve problems and achieve things that we could not do on our own.

◆ To enable the children to see that there are a range of skills involved in working as a group.

ANTICIPATED OUTCOMES

◆ They will understand the advantages of teamwork.
◆ They will be able to identify some of the things needed for effective teamwork to occur.

Synopsis of the story

Old Bear is threadbare and fragile and has been packed in a box and put into the attic for safe-keeping. Some time later, the rest of the toys, afraid that he had been forgotten, decide to go to his rescue. This is easier said than done, but by working together and trying out a variety of plans they eventually find a way of getting Old Bear out of the attic.

Notes for teachers

Getting children to see the advantages of working collaboratively is not always easy. Old Bear is an excellent story for helping them to see the benefits of working co-operatively.

The toys really work as a team, utilising the strengths of each individual. They work together to generate ideas and everyone's ideas are tried out. Together, they accomplish a task that would not otherwise have been possible and their ultimate satisfaction at having worked as a successful team is very evident.

Old Bear can also help the children in understanding the importance of persevering when things don't work out straight away. The toys have several failed attempts at getting Old Bear out of the attic before they eventually succeed.

Methodology

The following key questions and points for consideration may be helpful in exploring the issues raised in the story.

Questions to ask

- To help the children to understand how one person's initial idea may be developed through the contributions of others, ask: "Who first thought of the idea of getting Old Bear down from the attic? Could Bramwell Brown have done this on his own?"
- To understand how, in a group situation, we bounce ideas off each other, ask: "Little Bear suggested that they made a tower of bricks to get to the attic but the idea didn't work. What happened then?"
- Rabbit suggests that they all bounce on the bed as a way of reaching the attic but when it doesn't work, Duck becomes very upset. It is at this point in the story that Bramwell Brown really emerges as the leader of the team. To help the children to understand this ask: "When all their ideas had failed and Duck got very upset, who encouraged them to keep going?"
- It is important for the children to appreciate that the leader is only one part of a successful team. To help them understand this ask them to focus on the part played by other characters.
- Bramwell Brown has the idea of using the aeroplane. To help the children to understand the way in which the other toys build on and contribute to the idea, ask them: "What does Rabbit offer to do? What idea does Little Bear have? What important question does Duck ask?"
- "How do you think Old Bear feels when he realises that all his friends have been trying to get him out of the attic?"
- Look at the last picture in the book. "What do you think the toys might be thinking now? How do you think they felt when they finally got Old Bear out of the attic?"

The photocopiable activity sheets

Do you need help? This sheet focuses on getting the children to see the difference between problems they can solve on their own and those that require the support of others. It requires no writing and can prompt much discussion.

Working together This activity requires much discussion and a small amount of writing. For children who are not yet writing independently it could be carried out as a group activity with an adult scribe.

Using everyone's skills This activity is all about teamwork and demands quite a considerable range of skills. It is intended for older children.

FURTHER READING

- Tom and Sam by Pat Hutchins (Puffin)
- John Brown, Rose and the Midnight Cat by Jenny Wagner (Puffin)

◆ Do you need help? ◆

◆ Cut out the pictures and sort them into two groups.

Group 1
Problems I could solve on my own.

Group 2
Problems with which I would need other people's help.

Hopscotch ◆ Dealing with problems KS1/P1–3   PHOTOCOPIABLE PAGE   33

◆ Working together ◆

- How could these children work together to get the ball out of the tree?
- Write your ideas in the speech bubbles.

◆ Using everyone's skills ◆

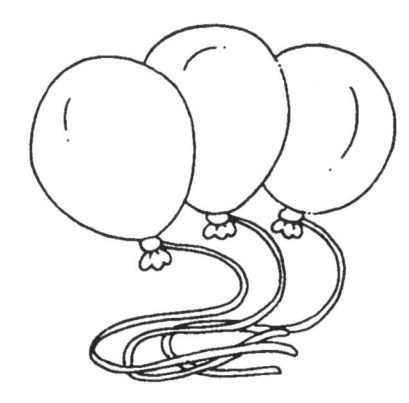

◆ Imagine that it is a friend's birthday and you are going to give them a surprise party.

◆ Talk with some friends and decide who would do what.

◆ Write a list of tasks for each person.

	Person 1	Person 2	Person 3	Person 4
Name				
Jobs				

◆ Tell the rest of the class about how you would plan and organise this party.

Hopscotch ◆ Dealing with problems KS1/P1–3   PHOTOCOPIABLE PAGE

◆ Making difficult choices

FOCUS BOOK

THE RAINBOW FISH
by Marcus Pfister
Nord-Sud

INTENDED LEARNING

◆ To help children understand that we cannot always have things the way we want them and that within relationships it is necessary to maintain a balance of giving and receiving.

ANTICIPATED OUTCOMES

◆ To understand that their own desires must be balanced and considered and that this sometimes results in the need to make difficult choices.

Synopsis of the story

The rainbow fish is a very simple but powerful story about a fish who is covered in shining scales and thinks himself far too beautiful to play with any of the other fish. When a little blue fish asks for one of his scales he is outraged and immediately refuses, with the consequence that all the other fish swim away and leave him on his own. It is not until he takes the difficult decision to part with his shining scales that the other fish become his friends. By the end of the story he has only one shining scale left but as he swims off to play with the other fish he is the happiest fish in the sea.

This book is available both as a board book and a big book.

Notes for teachers

By the time the children start school they are beginning to understand that life cannot always be just the way they would like it to be. This is a difficult thing to learn for all of us and coming to terms with the way in which we sometimes have to make difficult choices and decisions can be even more difficult. This is not easy for children and they need our support in accepting that in the process of daily life we are often required to make difficult choices and decisions.

When circumstances aren't just as children might wish them to be it is easy for them to see themselves as victims and feel frustrated and resentful. As adults, we may not be able to change children's circumstances but what we can do is to help them approach difficult situations in a positive way. By spending time reflecting on how we deal with difficult choices we can enable children to see that it is through such experiences that we grow and develop as people.

The Rainbow Fish provides us with an excellent platform for exploring the subtle relationship between giving and receiving. It also enables us to look at issues around sharing and generosity and question the appropriateness of having feelings of superiority.

Methodology

The following key questions and points for consideration may prove helpful when discussing this story.

Questions to ask

- To set the scene for discussion, ask: "How was the Rainbow Fish different from the other fish? Why didn't he play with the other fish? What words would you use to describe the way the Rainbow Fish felt about himself?" (This would be a good opportunity to introduce words like vain, conceited and self important.)
- Why do you think that the little blue fish wanted one of the Rainbow Fish's shining scales?
- Why did the Rainbow Fish laugh when the little blue fish asked for a scale?
- When the Rainbow Fish refused to give the little blue fish a scale, all the other fishes swam away from him. Why do you think this happened? Can you think of some words to describe how he felt when this happened? (Try to expand the children's feelings vocabulary as much as possible so that it extends beyond sad, upset and lonely. Introduce words such as isolated, dejected, rejected and confused).
- The Rainbow Fish went to the octopus for help and she told him to give away his shining scales. Why did she tell him to do this? Why did he not want to do it?
- The Rainbow Fish finally gives the little blue fish just one shining scale and the little blue fish is very happy, which makes the Rainbow Fish feel happy. Why do you think he felt happy?
- Encourage the children to relate the story to their own experience. Ask them: "Have you ever done something for somebody that has made them feel very happy?"
- The Rainbow Fish gave away all his scales except one and then he was very happy. Can you explain what made him feel so happy?
- In this story the Rainbow Fish had to make a difficult decision. Have you ever had to do this? (To get the discussion going you may have to give the children a few more examples. They enjoy it if we share our own experiences with them.)

The photocopiable activity sheets

What will you share? This is a simple activity about sharing that requires no writing and is intended for younger children.

What will happen? In this activity the children are asked to reflect upon a suitable ending to a simple story. Will the children leave Dad to do the washing-up on his own or will they go out to play? The sheet requires a small amount of writing but could also be done as an oral activity. Some well-focused discussion will help the children in making a responsible decision about how the story might end.

What will she do? This sheet calls for much thought and reflection. It requires the children to write independently and is intended for older children.

◆ What will you share? ◆

◆ Draw pictures to show some of the things that you would share with your friends.

What will happen?

◆ Choose a picture to finish the story.

◆ Which picture did you choose? Why?

PHOTOCOPIABLE PAGE

Hopscotch ◆ Dealing with problems KS1/P1–3

◆ What will she do? ◆

Come to the park with me!

No, don't do that. Come to my house and play on the computer!

◆ This girl has a very difficult choice to make.
◆ Think about what she could do and write what she should say to her friends.

Taking responsibility

FOCUS BOOK

IT WAS JAKE!
by Anita Jeram
Walker Books

INTENDED LEARNING

◆ To help children see the importance of taking responsibility for their own actions.

ANTICIPATED OUTCOMES

◆ They will recognise and talk about situations where they have blamed others for something that they have done. They will be able to suggest alternative ways of how they might have dealt with such situations.

Synopsis of the story

Danny and his dog Jake are always together but unfortunately, when Danny gets into mischief, it is Jake that gets the blame. This happens time and time again until Danny's Mum finally challenges him about it and sends him to bed without any supper. Danny finally acknowledges what he has done and, because he is really sorry for having been naughty, his Mum relents and takes him a glass of milk and some toast. Then while Danny is getting ready for bed, Jake finally has his revenge. When Danny gets into bed to eat his toast he finds that it has disappeared.

Notes for teachers

Taking responsibility for our own actions is not always easy and when things go wrong it is sometimes easier to dump the blame for what has happened onto someone or something else.

When children have done something wrong, made a mistake or in some way fallen short of the expectations of adults, they are faced with a difficult dilemma. They cannot always predict how adults will respond to them and may fear rejection as a consequence of what they have done. They may be afraid that their actions will provoke aggression, or that the adults will stop liking and respecting them, for being less than perfect.

If children are to learn to take responsibility for their own actions, they need a degree of tolerance and understanding from us. In order that they can acknowledge their own mistakes, it is necessary for them to understand that we are all thoughtless and get things wrong some of the time.

Exploring the issues raised in It Was Jake! can really help children to see that when we have made a mess of things the best thing we can do is take responsibility for what we have done and do our best to make amends.

Methodology

The following key questions and points for consideration may be helpful.

Questions to ask

- It may be helpful to begin by clarifying the relationship between Danny and his dog. Ask: "Why was Jake so special to Danny?"
- To ensure that they have grasped the focus of the story, ask: "When Danny decided to dress up, what did he do that annoyed his mother? Why do you think he tried to blame what happened on Jake?"
- Danny goes outside and decides to dig for buried treasure. Was this a good thing for him to do? If not, why not?
- Danny put Jake in the wash basin and when he heard his Mum coming he shouted Mum, look what Jake did! Why did he do this? Do you think that he knew that what he was doing was wrong? How can you tell?
- When Danny was cutting out, he made a terrible mess. How could he have avoided this? Again, Danny blamed Jake, was this fair? When Mum blames Danny for making all the mess, how do you think he feels? Why does Mum suggest that he needs to apologise?
- At the end of the story Jake eats Danny's toast. Do you think that he knows this is wrong?
- Encourage the children to relate the story to their own experiences. Ask: "Have you ever blamed someone else for something you did? Why did you do this? Has anyone ever tried to blame you for something you didn't do? How do you feel when this happens? Why do you think that we sometimes try to blame other people for things we have done? Why is it important for us to take responsibility for what we have done and own up to our mistakes? Can you get things right, or be good, all of the time? What is the most responsible thing to do when you have behaved badly or thoughtlessly?"

The photocopiable activity sheets

The accident This sheet is intended for younger children and is aimed at getting them thinking about what constitutes an 'accident' as opposed to what things are done deliberately. They can use their developmental writing here.

What should they do? This activity focuses on cause and effect and asks the children to consider what should be done in response to an accident. They should work in pairs to discuss each point before deciding what should be done. No writing is required but less developed children may need some support to read the prompts.

Who is to blame? This sheet requires the children to be able to engage in discussion with a friend and carry out a piece of independent writing. It is aimed at older or more able children.

◆ The accident ◆

◆ Look at this picture. What has happened?

◆ Draw a different picture about an accident.
Write some words about it.

Hopscotch ◆ Dealing with problems KS1/P1–3   PHOTOCOPIABLE PAGE

◆ What should they do? ◆

◆ Read these sentences. Put a ✔ or a ✘.

◆ The children should run away and hide. ☐

◆ The children should say sorry for what happened. ☐

◆ The children should use some of their pocket money to help pay for the window. ☐

◆ The children should say it wasn't them. ☐

◆ The children should say it was an accident. ☐

◆ The children should find a safer place to play. ☐

◆ Who is to blame? ◆

◆ Talk about this story with a friend. Answer the following questions in sentences.

◆ Who is to blame for what happened?

✎ _____

◆ What should the children do about what happened?

✎ _____
_____
_____
_____
_____

◆ Five facts about problems ◆

◆ Colour this poster and put it somewhere where you can come back and look at it when you have a problem.

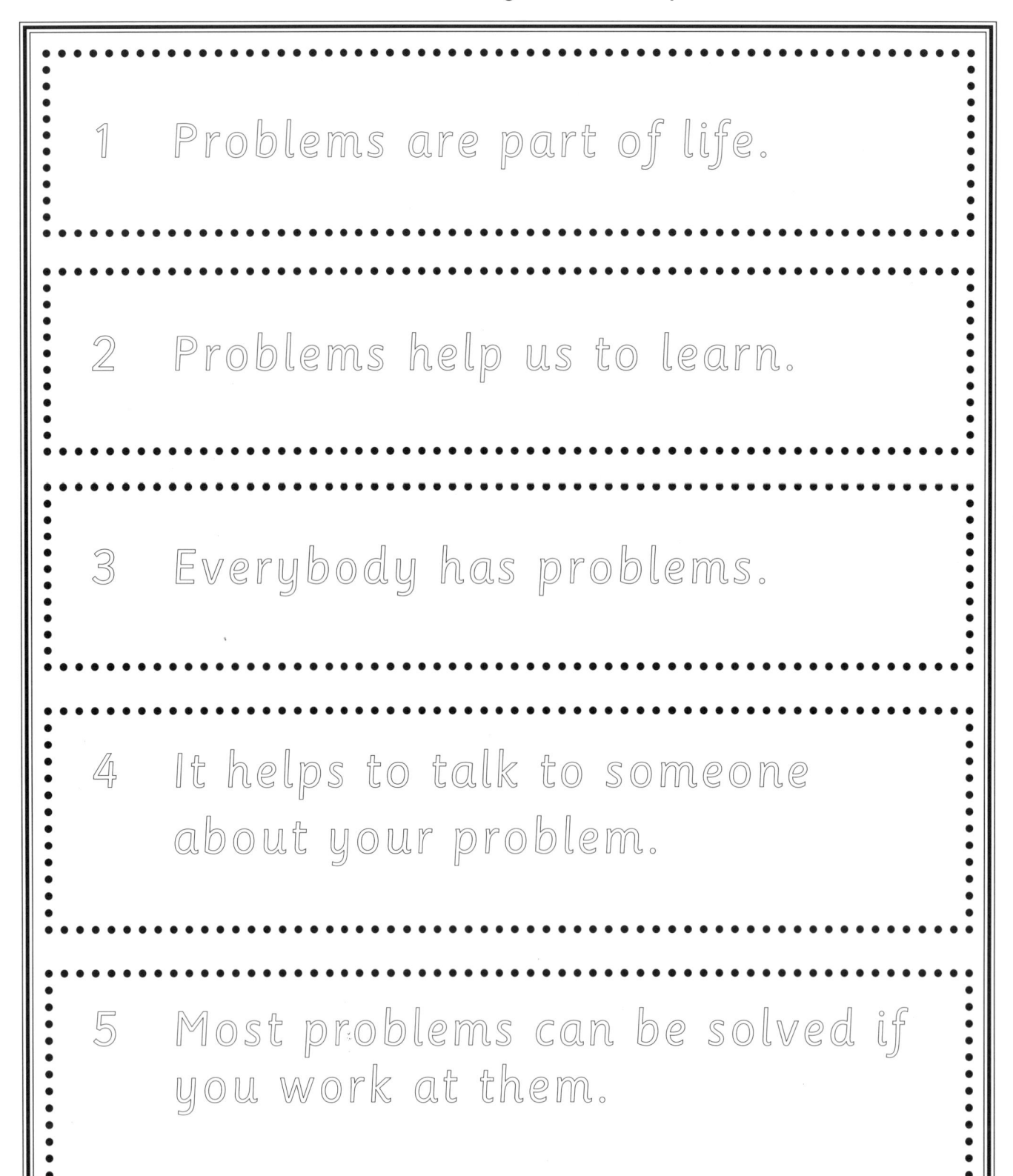

1   Problems are part of life.

2   Problems help us to learn.

3   Everybody has problems.

4   It helps to talk to someone about your problem.

5   Most problems can be solved if you work at them.

◆ Our problems ◆

◆ Talk to five of your friends and find out what causes them problems. Write their answers in the balloons.

◆ Compare your sheet with someone else. Have you got any answers that are the same?

Hopscotch ◆ Dealing with problems KS1/P1–3   PHOTOCOPIABLE PAGE   47

Acknowledgements

The following is a list of all the children's storybooks that have been referred to in this book as the basis for work on Personal, Moral, Social and Culural Education. The activities in this book can be be done using other storybooks.

- **Tall Inside** by Jean Richardson and Alice Englander (Picture Puffins)

- **Pass It, Polly** by Sarah Garland (Puffin)

- **Jamaica and Brianna** by Juanita Havill and Anne Sibley O'Brien (Mammoth)

- **Hector's New Trousers** by Amanda Vesey (Picture Lions)

- **Amazing Grace** by Mary Hoffman and Caroline Birch (Frances Lincoln)

- **Old Bear** by Jane Hissey (Arrow Books)

- **The Rainbow Fish** by Marcus Pfister (Nord-Sud, Verlag AG Gossau, Zurich)

- **It Was Jake!** by Anita Jeram (Walker Books)